飞鸟集

Stray Birds

〔印度〕罗宾德拉纳特·泰戈尔 著

冯唐 译

浙江出版联合集团
浙江文艺出版社

目 录

夏日的飞鸟来到我窗前　　　　　1.
歌
笑
翩跹
消失在我眼前

秋天的黄叶一直在窗前
无歌
无笑
无翩跹
坠落在我眼前

Stray birds of summer come to my window
to sing and fly away.
And yellow leaves of autumn, which have
no songs, flutter and fall there with a
sigh.

O Troupe of little vagrants of the world, leave
your footprints in my words.

2.

现世里孤孤单单的小混蛋啊

混到我的文字里留下你们的痕迹吧

The world puts off its mask of vastness to its
lover.
It becomes small as one song, as one kiss of the
eternal.

3.

大千世界在情人面前解开裤裆

绵长如舌吻

纤细如诗行

4.　　大地的泪水让笑脸常开不败

　　如花

　　如她

It is the tears of the earth
that keep her smiles in bloom.

大漠因为迷恋一叶绿草而焦黄

草摇

草笑

草跑

The mighty desert is burning for the love
of a blade of grass who shakes her head and
laughs and flies away.

6.

如果因为思念太阳而终日哭泣

星星也将离你而去

If you shed tears when you miss the sun,
you also miss the stars.

你旅途中的沙渴望随着你的歌唱出发

欢快的流水啊

你愿意背负沙的笨拙吗

The sands in your way beg for your song and your movement,
dancing water. Will you carry the burden of their lameness?

Her wistful face haunts my dreams
like the rain at night.

8.   她期待的脸萦绕我的梦

       雨落进夜的城

Once we dreamt that we were strangers.

We wake up to find that we were dear to each other.

做梦时　　　　　　　　　　9.

我们距离非常遥远

醒来时

我们在彼此的视野里取暖

Sorrow is hushed into peace in my heart like the
evening among the silent trees.

10.   痛在我心里渐渐平和
        夜在树林里一字不说

Some unseen fingers, like an idle breeze,
are playing upon my heart the music of the ripples.

看不见的手指   11.

无所事事的风

敲打我的心

响起水波间的音

"What language is thine, O sea?"

"The language of eternal question."

"What language is thy answer, O sky?"

"The language of eternal silence."

12.　　　"沧海，你用的是哪种语言？"

"永不止息的探问。"

"苍天，你用的是哪种语言？"

"永不止息的沉默。"

Listen, my heart, to the whispers of the world
with which it makes love to you.

心呐

听吧

这世界和你做爱的细碎响声啊

The mystery of creation is like the darkness of
night—it is great. Delusions of knowledge are like
the fog of the morning.

14.   创造的隐秘

           夜晚无穷无尽的黑暗

           已知的虚幻

           早晨的雾气飞快消散

Do not seat your love upon a precipice because it is
high.

不要将爱托付给悬崖　　　　15.
只是因为悬崖够高啊

16.　新的一天
　　　　我坐在窗前
　　　　世界如过客
　　　　在我面前走过
　　　　停了
　　　　点头
　　　　又走了

I sit at my window this morning where the world like
a passer-by stops for a moment, nods to me and goes.

这些小小的心思

娑娑响的叶子

我心里欢喜不止

These little thoughts are the rustle of leaves; they
have their whisper of joy in my mind.

What you are you do not see,
what you see is your shadow.

18.   你无法看到自己
      你看到的是你认为的自己

My wishes are fools, they shout across thy songs,
my Master.
Let me but listen.

神啊

我的欲念如此纷纷扰扰呆痴憨傻

好吧

我只是听听吧

I cannot choose the best.
The best chooses me.

20.   我做不到选择最好的
        是最好的选择了我

They throw their shadows before them who carry their
lantern on their back.

将灯背在身后的人

阴影在他们面前延伸

That I exist is a perpetual surprise which is life.

22.　　　我存在
　　　　是生命绵延不断的精彩

"We, the rustling leaves, have a voice that answers the storms, but who are you so silent?"

"I am a mere flower."

"我们是沙沙作响的叶子

对狂风啊

我们沙沙

你谁啊，不说一句话？"

"我只是一枝花。"

23.

Rest belongs to the work as the eyelids to the eyes.

24.　　　劳作之后休憩

　　　　　眼帘盖住眼底

Man is a born child, his power is the power of growth.

人类永远只是孩子   25.

他的力量只是生长的力量

God expects answers for the flowers he sends us, not
for the sun and the earth.

26.　　　神在等待我们答题

　　　　对于他开出的花朵

　　　　不是对于他开出的天与地

The light that plays, like a naked child, among the
green leaves happily knows not that man can lie.

光玩耍着绿色的叶子   27.

如同一个光着的孩子

懵然不知世间有很多骗子

O Beauty, find thyself in love,
not in the flattery of thy mirror.

28.　　　美

在爱中

不在镜中

My heart beats her waves at the shore of the world and writes upon it her signature in tears with the words,"I love thee."

我的心起伏在尘世的岸边 29.

用泪水签下印记

“我爱你”

"Moon, for what do you wait?"
"To salute the sun for whom I must make way."

30.　　　　"月亮，为什么你在等待？"

　　　　"我等着给太阳致敬，然后离开。"

The trees come up to my window like the yearning
voice of the dumb earth.

树枝伸进我的窗　　　　　　　31.
大地无声的渴望

His own mornings are new surprises to God.

32.   对于自己创造的清晨

       神自己都充满惊奇

Life finds its wealth by the claims of the world, and
its worth by the claims of love.

从世所愿   33.

生命有了金钱

从爱所愿

生命有了金线

The dry river-bed finds no thanks for its past.

34.   干枯的河床

        不感谢过去的时光

The bird wishes it were a cloud.
The cloud wishes it were a bird.

飞鸟希望自己是云彩   35.

云彩希望自己是飞鸟

36.   瀑布流淌：

　　　　"自由之后

　　　　才有歌唱。"

The waterfall sings,
"I find my song,
when I find my freedom."

我不知道

37.

这心为什么在寂寞中枯焦

为了那些细小的需要
从没说要
从不明了
总想忘掉

I cannot tell why this heart languishes in silence.
It is for small needs it never asks, or knows or
remembers.

Woman, when you move about in your household
service your limbs sing like a hill stream among
its pebbles.

38.　　　姑娘
　　　　你在你屋子里忙
　　　　你的手臂像泉水在山石间流淌

The sun goes to cross the Western sea, leaving
its last salutation to the East.

太阳将巡西洋

将最后的敬礼留给东方

Do not blame your food because you have no appetite.

40.　　　没食欲的时候

　　　　不要责备你的食物

The trees, like the longings of the earth, stand
a-tiptoe to peep at the heaven.

树

大地的渴望

踮着脚偷窥天堂

41.

42. 你对我微笑不语

为这句我等了几个世纪

You smiled and talked to me of nothing and I felt
that for this I had been waiting long.

鱼寂海上　　　　　43.
兽噪地上
鸟鸣天上

人同时拥有
海的静寂
地的肉欲
天的神曲

The fish in the water is silent,
the animal on the earth is noisy,
the bird in the air is singing.
But Man has in him the silence of the sea,
the noise of the earth and the music of the air.

44.　　　世界踏着心的琴弦匆匆而过

　　　　低徊的心唱了很久忧伤的歌

The world rushes on over the strings of the
lingering heart making the music of sadness.

他尊他的剑为神　　　　　　　　45.

剑胜了

他输了

He has made his weapons his gods.

When his weapons win he is defeated himself.

46.　　　　神在创造中发现自己

God finds himself by creating.

戴着面纱的影子　　　　　　　　47.

随着光的步子

爱恋

柔软

Shadow, with her veil drawn,

follows Light in secret meekness,

with her silent steps of love.

48.   星星

不在乎看上去像秋萤

The stars are not afraid to appear like fireflies.

我感恩   49.

我不是权力的车轮

我只是被车轮碾碎的某个鲜活的人

I thank thee that I am none of the wheels of power

but I am one with the living creatures

that are crushed by it.

50.　　　　那些尖锐而不广博的心性

　　　　执泥而一无所成

The mind, sharp but not broad, sticks at every
point but does not move.

你的偶像坍塌成尘土 51.

神的尘土大于你的偶像

Your idol is shattered in the dust to prove that
God's dust is greater than your idol.

52.　　　人在历史里湮没无闻
　　　　人总是努力超越现存

Man does not reveal himself in his history, he
struggles up through it.

陶土灯叫他表兄

玻璃灯不高兴

夜来月升

玻璃灯满脸笑容

"我亲爱的，亲爱的姐妹。"

While the glass lamp rebukes the earthen
for calling it cousin, the moon rises,
and the glass lamp,
with a bland smile, calls her,——
"My dear, dear sister."

54.　　　　我们走近

　　　　　　海鸥和海浪相亲

　　　　　　海鸥飞起

　　　　　　海浪翻去

　　　　　　我们分离

Like the meeting of the seagulls
and the waves we meet and come near.
The seagulls fly off,
the waves roll away and we depart.

日间劳作完

我如一条瘫软在岸的船

听浪的舞曲回荡在夜晚

My day is done,

and I am like a boat drawn on the beach,

listening to the dance-music of the tide

in the evening.

56.　　　　天予我们生命
　　　　　我们献出生命
　　　　　从而获得生命

Life is given to us, we earn it by giving it.

我们最谦和的时候   57.

是我们最伟大的时候

We come nearest to the great when we are great in
humility.

58.　　　麻雀认为

　　　　　孔雀的尾巴真是累赘

The sparrow is sorry for the peacock at the burden
of its tail.

永恒的声音吟唱道   59.

不要害怕那些瞬间

Never be afraid of the moments—thus sings the voice
of the everlasting.

60.　　　台风在无路之路

　　　　走最便捷的近路

　　　　止于最荒芜之处

The hurricane seeks the shortest road by the no-road,
and suddenly ends its search in the Nowhere.

请用我的杯子
喝我的酒
朋友

如果倒进别人的杯子
它就是另外一个样子

Take my wine in my own cup, friend.
It loses its wreath of foam when poured into that of
others.

The Perfect decks itself in beauty for the love of
the Imperfect.

62. 完美
因为深爱不完美
把自己打扮得很美

God says to man, "I heal you therefore I hurt, love
you therefore punish."

神对人说 63.

我治愈所以我鞭打

我爱你所以我惩罚

Thank the flame for its light, but do not forget the
lampholder standing in the shade with constancy of
patience.

64.　　　　感恩光明

但是别忘了是谁

长久地在黑暗中擎起了那盏灯

Tiny grass, your steps are small, but you possess
the earth under your tread.

小草   65.

脚步虽小

脚下有大地

The infant flower opens its bud and cries,
"Dear World, please do not fade."

66.　　　初开的花蕾叫道：

　　　"亲爱的世界，

　　　不要凋谢。"

God grows weary of great kingdoms,
but never of little flowers.

神总是厌倦那些伟大的王国   67.
神从不厌倦任何小小的花朵

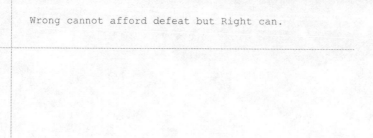

Wrong cannot afford defeat but Right can.

68.　　　　谬误受不了任何失败

　　　　　但是真理不怕

"I give my whole water in joy," sings the waterfall,
"though little of it is enough for the thirsty."

瀑布唱道   69.
我乐得给出我所有的水
虽然你解渴只需一小杯

Where is the fountain that throws up these flowers in
a ceaseless outbreak of ecstasy?

70.　　　无止地

　　　　狂喜地

　　　　射出那么多花朵

　　　　这力量的源头到底在哪儿呢？

The woodcutter's axe begged for its handle from the tree.

The tree gave it.

砍树的铁斧向树要木头把儿   71.

树给了它

In my solitude of heart I feel the sigh of this
widowed evening veiled with mist and rain.

72.　　　　在我心的枯寂中
　　　　　我听到夜的叹息
　　　　　雾
　　　　　雨

Chastity is a wealth
that comes from abundance of love.

爱满了   73.

就没空地儿花心了

The mist, like love, plays upon the heart of the
hills and brings out surprises of beauty.

74.　　　　此时的雾

　　　　　如爱

　　　　　和山峦的心游戏

　　　　　变幻出各种瑰丽

We read the world wrong and say that it deceives us.

我们没读明白尘世
却说尘世是个骗子

75.

76.　　　在海和树林

　　　　　有诗人的风吹起

　　　　　在找自己的声音

The poet wind is out over the sea
and the forest to seek his own voice.

每个婴儿都带着同一个讯息   77.
"神还没对人类彻底失去信心"

Every child comes with the message
that God is not yet discouraged of man.

78.   草在地上凑热闹

       树在天空求孤独

The grass seeks her crowd in the earth.
The tree seeks his solitude of the sky.

人类擅长　　　　79.
设卡自防

Man barricades against himself.

80.　　　你的声音

　　　在我心上

　　　低低的海声

　　　在倾听的松

Your voice, my friend, wanders in my heart, like the
muffled sound of the sea among these listening pines.

什么是暗夜看不见的火焰

星星是它溅出的残片

What is this unseen flame of darkness whose sparks

are the stars?

82.　　　愿生命灿若夏花

　　　　愿死亡美如秋叶

Let life be beautiful like summer flowers and death
like autumn leaves.

想做善事的人   83.

敲了敲门

爱满心房的人

自己敞开着门

He who wants to do good knocks at the gate; he who
loves finds the gate open.

84.   死时

　　　　众人变成同一个样子

　　　　生时

　　　　婴儿长成众多的样子

　　　　上帝死去

　　　　众教合一

In death the many becomes one;

in life the one becomes many.

Religion will be one when God is dead.

艺术家是自然的情人 85.
所以他既是她的奴隶又是她的主人

The artist is the lover of Nature,
therefore he is her slave and her master.

86.　　　　"果实，你离我还有多遥远？"

　　　　　"花朵，我一直藏在你心间。"

"How far are you from me, O Fruit?"

"I am hidden in your heart, O Flower."

某种渴望只为某个人　　　　　87.
暗夜里感觉到她
白昼里见不到她

This longing is for the one who is felt in the dark,
but not seen in the day.

88.　　　"你是莲叶下面最大一颗露水

我是莲叶上面最小一颗露水。"

露水告诉湖水

"You are the big drop of dew under the lotus leaf,
I am the smaller one on its upper side," said the
dewdrop to the lake.

剑鞘满足于自身的钝

保护了宝剑锋利的刃

The scabbard is content to be dull when it protects
the keenness of the sword.

90.　　　　在黑暗中

　　　　　太一似一

　　　　　在光亮中

　　　　　太一似亿

In darkness the One appears as uniform; in the light
the One appears as manifold.

有了绿草

大地变得挺骚

The great earth makes herself hospitable with the
help of the grass.

92.　　　　树叶的生灭

　　　　　旋涡快速的旋转

　　　　　星星的明暗

　　　　　旋涡宽缓的旋转

The birth and death of the leaves are the rapid
whirls of the eddy whose wider circles move slowly
among stars.

强权对世界说:

"你丫是我的。"

世界让强权变成王座的囚徒

爱情对世界说:

"我呀是你的。"

世界让爱情在世上任意飞舞

Power said to the world,

"You are mine."

The world kept it prisoner on her throne.

Love said to the world,

"I am thine."

The world gave it the freedom of her house.

94.　　　雾

大地的欲望

藏起了太阳

哭得忧伤

The mist is like the earth's desire.
It hides the sun for whom she cries.

我的心啊   95.

平静些吧

这些大树都是祈祷者啊

Be still, my heart, these great trees are prayers.

The noise of the moment scoffs at the music of the Eternal.

96.　　此时的噪音

嘲笑永恒的乐音

I think of other ages that floated upon the stream
of life and love and death and are forgotten,
and I feel the freedom of passing away.

那些时代

那些被忘记的时代

那些在生与爱与死的长河上漂流的时代

想着想着

我不怕死了

The sadness of my soul is her bride's veil.
It waits to be lifted in the night.

98.   我消魂的黯然是新娘的面纱
        等夜晚到来之后再摘下

Death's stamp gives value to the coin of life;
making it possible to buy with life what is truly
precious.

死亡之印给生命的钱币定价

以此购买真正宝贵的生命之花

The cloud stood humbly in a corner of the sky.
The morning crowned it with splendour.

100.　　云谦卑地立在天边

　　　　晨光给它戴上金冠

The dust receives insult and in return offers her flowers.

尘土包容羞辱

开出花骨朵儿

101.

102. 不要为了收集花朵而留步
      花朵也盛开在你前头

Do not linger to gather flowers to keep them, but
walk on, for flowers will keep themselves blooming
all your way.

根是地下的枝干　　　103.
枝干是地上的根

Roots are the branches down in the earth.
Branches are roots in the air.

The music of the far-away summer flutters around the
Autumn seeking its former nest.

104.　　远去的夏天的音乐

　　　　徘徊在秋夜

　　　　思念过去的巢穴

Do not insult your friend by lending him merits from your own pocket.

别借给别人你的好

那也是一种侮辱

The touch of the nameless days clings to my heart
like mosses round the old tree.

106.　　心里挥之不去的无名的日子

　　　　苔藓挽住老树的脖子

The echo mocks her origin to prove she is the
original.

回音嘲笑原声   107.
以此证明自己是原声

God is ashamed when the prosperous boasts of His
special favour.

108.　　　飞黄腾达的人号称有如神佑

神羞愧地低下了头

I cast my own shadow upon my path, because I have a
lamp that has not been lighted.

我自己的阴影遮在自己的路上   109.
因为我有盏自己的灯没有点亮

Man goes into the noisy crowd to drown his own
clamour of silence.

110.　　　人们融进人群的喧嚣
　　　　　为了消除内心的聒噪

That which ends in exhaustion is death, but the
perfect ending is in the endless.

耗尽了的尽头是死　　　　　　111.
圆满的尽头是不死

The sun has his simple robe of light. The clouds
are decked with gorgeousness.

112.　　　太阳只穿了光素的衣裳
　　　云彩披上了亮骚的大氅

The hills are like shouts of children who raise
their arms, trying to catch stars.

山峦像是孩子们的叫声   113.

孩子们伸出手臂

摘取星星

The road is lonely in its crowd for it is not loved.

114.　　　道路在拥挤中孤寂

　　　　它没感到一点爱意

The power that boasts of its mischiefs is laughed at
by the yellow leaves that fall, and clouds that pass
by.

强权因为可以胡作非为而得意   115.

落叶笑了

浮云飘了

116.　　　　今天大地在阳光下对我嘤嘤作响

　　　　　　织布的姑娘

　　　　　　死了的语言

　　　　　　远古的吟唱

The earth hums to me to-day in the sun, like a woman
at her spinning, some ballad of the ancient time in
a forgotten tongue.

草叶 117.
无愧于它所生长的世界

The grass-blade is worthy of the great world where
it grows.

118.　　　梦幻是一个不得不唠叨的老婆

　　　　　睡眠是一个默默忍受着的老公

Dream is a wife who must talk,
Sleep is a husband who silently suffers.

白日将尽

夜晚呢喃

"我是死啊，

我是你妈，

我会给你新生哒。"

The night kisses the fading day whispering to his
ear,"I am death, your mother. I am to give you fresh
birth."

120.　　　夜啊

　　　　　我能触摸到你的美啊

　　　　　仿佛恋爱中的女人

　　　　　吹灭了她的灯啊

I feel thy beauty,

dark night,

like that of the loved woman

when she has put out the lamp.

我把落败世界的荣光带到现世来

I carry in my world that flourishes the worlds that
have failed.

122.　　　听潮

　　　　黄昏渐消

　　　　我想我听懂了你伟大思想的寂寥

Dear friend, I feel the silence of your great
thoughts of many a deepening eventide on this beach
when I listen to these waves.

鸟觉得

它把鱼叼离海面

是积德行善

The bird thinks it is an act of kindness to give the
fish a lift in the air.

124.　　　　"你在月亮上寄给我情书，"

夜晚告诉太阳

"我用泪水答在草叶上。"

"In the moon thou sendest thy love letters to me," said
the night to the sun.
"I leave my answers in tears upon the grass."

大师注定都是孩子   125.
死时把伟大的孩子气留在世上

The Great is a born child; when he dies he gives his
great childhood to the world.

126.　　不是铁锤

而是流水

唱着跳着把鹅卵石变得异常完美

Not hammer-strokes, but dance of the water sings the
pebbles into perfection.

蜜蜂采蜜 127.
道谢辞花
浪蝶觉得花应该谢谢他

Bees sip honey from flowers and hum their thanks when
they leave.
The gaudy butterfly is sure that the flowers owe
thanks to him.

128.　　　真话不说全

　　　　　容易坦然

To be outspoken is easy when you do not wait to
speak the complete truth.

"皆有可能"问"没可能" 129.

"你住哪儿？"

"我住在无能者的梦中。"

Asks the Possible to the Impossible,

"Where is your dwelling-place?"

"In the dreams of the impotent," comes the answer.

130.　　　关上门

　　　　摒弃所有错误

　　　　真理也被堵住

If you shut your door to all errors truth will be
shut out.

我听见伤心处有细碎的声响　　　　　131.

我看不见他们

I hear some rustle of things behind my sadness of
heart,——I cannot see them.

132.　闲里动动就是做工
　　　海的安静微微晃晃就是浪

Leisure in its activity is work.
The stillness of the sea stirs in waves.

叶子灿烂开花

因为恋爱了

花朵丰满结果

因为崇拜了

The leaf becomes flower when it loves.
The flower becomes fruit when it worships.

134.　　　地上的枝结满水果

　　　　　地下的根不计功过

The roots below the earth claim no rewards for
making the branches fruitful.

夜雨下   135.
风乱刮
我静观摇曳的树枝
我静思所有事物的伟大

This rainy evening the wind is restless.
I look at the swaying branches and ponder over the
greatness of all things.

136.　　　午夜的风暴

　　　　　黑暗中被惊起的小孩

　　　　　开始叫

　　　　　开始玩

Storm of midnight, like a giant child awakened in
the untimely dark, has begun to play and shout.

海   137.

风暴孤独的新娘

徒劳地掀起波浪

追随她的新郎

Thou raisest thy waves vainly to follow thy lover, O
sea, thou lonely bride of the storm.

138.   词语对作品说

"我耻于我的空虚。"

作品对词语说

"我耻于我的贫瘠。"

"I am ashamed of my emptiness," said the Word to the
Work.
"I know how poor I am when I see you," said the Work
to the Word.

时光是变化的宝物   139.

时钟走动

只有变化

没有宝物

Time is the wealth of change, but the clock in its
parody makes it mere change and no wealth.

140.   真相穿上衣服
           事实让它局促
           真相钻进小说
           它自在了很多

Truth in her dress finds facts too tight.
In fiction she moves with ease.

去这儿去那儿的时光 141.

我厌倦了在路上

如今可以自由行走

我定了这辈子只在路上

When I travelled to here and to there, I was tired

of thee, O Road, but now when thou leadest me to

everywhere I am wedded to thee in love.

142.　　　　我宁愿这样盘算

群星中一定有一颗星星

领我走出生命中无名的黑暗

Let me think that there is one among those stars
that guides my life through the dark unknown.

美女   143.

你美美的指尖

安顿我的物件

完成的秩序如同神曲

Woman, with the grace of your fingers you touched my

things and order came out like music.

144.　　　一个忧郁的声音

筑巢于岁月的灰烬

晚上对我唱

"我爱过你"

One sad voice has its nest among the ruins of the years.
It sings to me in the night,——"I loved you."

火的光热不让我靠近   145.
让我远离将死的余烬

The flaming fire warns me off by its own glow.
Save me from the dying embers hidden under ashes.

146.　　　　我有我的繁星漫天
　　　　　　我房中的灯没点燃

I have my stars in the sky,
But oh for my little lamp unlit in my house.

纠缠你的旧文字的灰尘 147.

在安静中濯净你的灵魂

The dust of the dead words clings to thee.

Wash thy soul with silence.

148.　　生命中那些未了的事物

　　　　筛子一样漏出死的音符

Gaps are left in life through which comes the sad
music of death.

早晨的光芒

世界敞开的心房

我的心啊

带着爱见见它吧

The world has opened its heart of light in the
morning.
Come out, my heart, with thy love to meet it.

150.   树叶闪烁

我的念想闪烁

阳光触摸

我的心唱歌

我的生命与众生欣然同行

进入幽蓝的空间

进入黑寂的时间

My thoughts shimmer with these shimmering leaves and
my heart sings with the touch of this sunlight;
my life is glad to be floating with all things into
the blue of space, into the dark of time.

神的伟力   151.

在微风里

不在风暴里

God's great power is in the gentle breeze, not in
the storm.

152.   梦里
       所有事物松软
       所有事物侵染

       醒来
       所有事物聚集于你
       于是我自由于天地

This is a dream in which things are all loose and
they oppress. I shall find them gathered in thee when
I awake and shall be free.

"我去后，谁替我值班？"   153.

落日问

"主人啊，我尽我所能。"

陶灯答

"Who is there to take up my duties?" asked the
setting sun.
"I shall do what I can, my Master," said the
earthen lamp.

154.　　摘去花瓣

　　　　得不到花朵的美丽

By plucking her petals you do not gather the beauty
of the flower.

静寂盛了你的声音　　　　155.
鸟巢盛了睡着的鸟

Silence will carry your voice like the nest that
holds the sleeping birds.

The Great walks with the Small without fear.
The Middling keeps aloof.

156.

伟大不怕和渺小并肩而行

不上不下的总是孤芳自赏

The night opens the flowers in secret and allows
the day to get thanks.

暗夜   157.
悄悄打开花的笑靥
让白昼接受感谢

Power takes as ingratitude the writhings of its
victims.

158.　　在强权看来
　　　　牺牲品的痛苦是不知好歹

When we rejoice in our fulness, then we can part
with our fruits with joy.

花开
尽情盛开
果来
坦然离开

159.

The raindrops kissed the earth and whispered,——"We
are thy homesick children, mother, come back to thee
from the heaven."

160.　　雨滴亲吻大地:

　　　"我们是您想家的孩子

　　　从天上重回您的怀里。"

The cobweb pretends to catch dewdrops and catches
flies.

蛛网作势捉露珠
却捉住苍蝇

162.　　爱
　　　　手上燃着痛苦的灯
　　　　走来

　　　　我
　　　　看见你的面颊
　　　　知道你开心啊

Love! When you come with the burning lamp of pain
in your hand, I can see your face and know you as
bliss.

"根据学者研究   163.

终有一日你会黯淡无光"

萤火虫对星星讲

星星什么都没讲

"The learned say that your lights will one day be no
more," said the firefly to the stars.
The stars made no answer.

164.　　黄昏的微光中
　　　　一只早晨的飞鸟
　　　　回到我沉默的巢

In the dusk of the evening the bird of some early
dawn comes to the nest of my silence.

念想在脑里飞翔   165.

鸭子在天上飞翔

我听到它们翅膀的声响

Thoughts pass in my mind like flocks of ducks in the
sky.
I hear the voice of their wings.

166. 沟渠喜欢这样思维
大河的存在只是为它供水

The canal loves to think that rivers exist solely to
supply it with water.

世界用它的痛　　　　　　　167.

亲吻我的魂魄

让我还它以歌

The world has kissed my soul with its pain, asking
for its return in songs.

168.　　　是谁让我肿胀

是我的魂要离我而飞翔

还是世界的魂要进入我心房

That which oppresses me, is it my soul trying to
come out in the open, or the soul of the world
knocking at my heart for its entrance?

念想用自身的词汇供养　　　　　169.
自我生长

Thought feeds itself with its own words and grows.

170.　　　我将心房浸入此刻的时间之海

它盛了满满的爱

I have dipped the vessel of my heart into this
silent hour; it has filled with love.

你或者在做

或者没做

当你不得不说

"我们做点什么吧"

你就要做错了

Either you have work or you have not.

When you have to say,"Let us do something,"

then begins mischief.

172.   向日葵羞与
        无名小花为伍

        太阳升起
        笑问小花
        "亲爱的小花，你还好吗？"

The sunflower blushed to own the nameless flower as
her kin.
The sun rose and smiled on it, saying, "Are you well,
my darling?"

"是谁像命运一样催我向前？"

"是我自己一直在我后面。"

"Who drives me forward like fate?"
"The Myself striding on my back."

The clouds fill the watercups of the river, hiding
themselves in the distant hills.

174.   云把河的水杯斟满
          躲进远山

I spill water from my water jar as I walk on my way,
Very little remains for my home.

我的水罐一路滴答
回到家基本没水啦

176.　　　　罐子里的水灿烂
　　　　　　大海里的水暗淡

　　　　　　小常识能说清楚
　　　　　　大正见沉默望天

The water in a vessel is sparkling; the water in the
sea is dark.
The small truth has words that are clear; the great
truth has great silence.

你的微笑是你花园的花开

你的谈话是你松林的风来

但是你的心

是我们都熟知的那位女神

Your smile was the flowers of your own fields, your
talk was the rustle of your own mountain pines, but
your heart was the woman that we all know.

It is the little things that I leave behind for my
loved ones,——great things are for everyone.

178.　　　　细小的物件儿
　　　　　留给我深爱的人儿

　　　　　伟大的物件儿
　　　　　留给所有人

Woman, thou hast encircled the world's heart with
the depth of thy tears as the sea has the earth.

女人啊   179.
用泪拥抱尘世的心
如同大海包裹陆地

The sunshine greets me with a smile.

The rain, his sad sister, talks to my heart.

180.　　　阳光微笑迎我

雨

它忧伤的妹妹

和我的心说话

My flower of the day dropped its petals forgotten.

In the evening it ripens into a golden fruit of memory.

我的花在白天　　　　　　　　181.

忘记了零落成泥的花瓣

我的花在夜晚

圆熟成金黄的记忆之果

I am like the road in the night listening to the
footfalls of its memories in silence.

182.　　　我如同夜晚的道路
　　　　在静寂中听着记忆的脚步

The evening sky to me is like a window, and a
lighted lamp, and a waiting behind it.

对于我   183.

夜空是

一扇窗

一豆灯

灯后有什么在等

He who is too busy doing good finds no time to be good.

184.　　　一个太忙着做好事的人
　　　　发现自己没时间做好人

I am the autumn cloud, empty of rain, see my fulness
in the field of ripened rice.

我是秋天的云   185.

空洞无雨

我的满足来自田里成熟的米

They hated and killed and men praised them.
But God in shame hastens to hide its memory under
the green grass.

186.　　他们仇恨

　　　　他们杀人

　　　　人们赞美他们

　　　　神羞得尽快用绿草掩埋记忆

Toes are the fingers that have forsaken their past.

脚趾是摒弃了过去的手指　　　187.

Darkness travels towards light, but blindness
towards death.

188.   黑暗走向光芒
        盲者走向死亡

The pet dog suspects the universe for scheming to
take its place.

宠物狗怀疑全世界都要取代它的位置   189.

Sit still, my heart, do not raise your dust.
Let the world find its way to you.

190.　　　安静坐稳

　　　　　我的心

　　　　　不要扬起你的尘

　　　　　让世界自己敲响你的门

The bow whispers to the arrow before it speeds
forth——"Your freedom is mine."

弓在放箭之前

小声对箭说

"你的自由是我的"

192.　女人啊

你的笑声

有生命之泉的乐声

Woman, in your laughter you have the music of the
fountain of life.

全是逻辑的大脑

没鞘的刀

谁用谁伤

A mind all logic is like a knife all blade.
It makes the hand bleed that uses it.

194.   神爱人的灯光
        胜于爱它自己的星光

God loves man's lamp lights better than his own
great stars.

此世界

是被美之音乐

驯服了的狂风暴雨的世界

This world is the world of wild storms kept tame
with the music of beauty.

196.　　　"我的心

　　　　像金色宝盒

　　　　装了你的吻"

　　　　暮云对太阳说

"My heart is like the golden casket of thy kiss,"
said the sunset cloud to the sun.

摸了

就破了

远着

就一直有着

By touching you may kill, by keeping away you may
possess.

198.　蟋蟀唧唧

　　　　夜雨沥沥

　　　　趁着黑

　　　　过去的青春来到我的梦里

The cricket's chirp and the patter of rain come to
me through the dark, like the rustle of dreams from
my past youth.

"我失去了我的朝露"

花朵对曙空哭

曙空失去了它所有的星星

"I have lost my dewdrop," cries the flower to the
morning sky that has lost all its stars.

200.　　　　燃烧的木头迸发火光

　　　　　"这是我的花啊，我的死亡"

The burning log bursts in flame and cries,—"This is
my flower, my death."

大黄蜂认为隔壁蜜蜂的蜂巢太小了

蜜蜂让它做个更小的

The wasp thinks that the honeyhive of the
neighbouring bees is too small.
His neighbours ask him to build one still smaller.

202.　　　"我留不住你的波浪"

河岸对河流说

"那就让我在心里留住你的脚印吧"

"I cannot keep your waves," says the bank to the
river.
"Let me keep your footprints in my heart."

白昼 　　　　　　　　　　　　　　　203.

小小地球的熙熙攘攘
淹没了其他万千世界的悠扬

The day, with the noise of this little earth, drowns
the silence of all worlds.

204.   歌无极

　　　在空气里

　　　画无极

　　　在大地上

　　　诗无极

　　　在空气和大地

　　　诗的字句里

　　　有能流传的意义

　　　有能翱翔的乐音

The song feels the infinite in the air, the picture
in the earth, the poem in the air and the earth;
For its words have meaning that walks and music that
soars.

太阳沉于西方之瞬间   205.

早晨的东方已静立在面前

When the sun goes down to the West, the East of his
morning stands before him in silence.

206.　　我不要把自我错置在我的天地

　　　　我不让自我与我为敌

Let me not put myself wrongly to my world and set it
against me.

赞赏让我蒙羞

因为我暗中对它渴求

Praise shames me, for I secretly beg for it.

208.　　当我无所事事时

　　　　请让我在深深的从容中无所事事

　　　　仿佛水波不兴的岸边的漫漫长夜

Let my doing nothing when I have nothing to do
become untroubled in its depth of peace like the
evening in the seashore when the water is silent.

姑娘
你的简单
仿佛湖水的碧蓝
彰显真理的绚烂

Maiden, your simplicity, like the blueness of the
lake, reveals your depth of truth.

210.   最好的事物从不独来
        它从来伴着一切而来

The best does not come alone.
It comes with the company of the all.

神的右手菩萨
但是左手恶煞

God's right hand is gentle, but terrible is his left
hand.

My evening came among the alien trees and spoke in a
language which my morning stars did not know.

212.　　　我的夜在陌生的林中落下
　　　　　说着我的晨星听不懂的话

Night's darkness is a bag that bursts with the gold
of the dawn.

夜的黑暗的袋子

漏出晨光细碎的金子

Our desire lends the colours of the rainbow to the
mere mists and vapours of life.

214.   我们的欲望
        把彩虹的七色宝光
        借给生命中的虚妄

God waits to win back his own flowers as gifts from
man's hands.

神静候从人的手上赢回自己的花   215.

多好的礼物啊

216.　　　　我无尽的忧伤

　　　　　　不停地鼓动我

　　　　　　问它们叫什么

My sad thoughts tease me asking me their own names.

水果的奉献是宝贵的

花朵的奉献是甜美的

让我的奉献如树荫吧

卑微的，一心一意的

The service of the fruit is precious, the service
of the flower is sweet, but let my service be
the service of the leaves in its shade of humble
devotion.

My heart has spread its sails to the idle winds for
the shadowy island of Anywhere.

218.　　　我的心张开帆

　　　　　借着无所事事的风

　　　　　去无所谓哪里的岛

Men are cruel, but Man is kind.

庸众是残酷的 219.

每个人是善良的

Make me thy cup and let my fulness be for thee and
for thine.

220.   把我当作你的杯子吧

我盛满了

都是为你

都是你的

The storm is like the cry of some god in pain whose
love the earth refuses.

暴风雨   221.
神痛苦的哭泣
因为大地拒绝了它的爱

The world does not leak because death is not a
crack.

222.　　　世界疏而不漏

死亡一个不落

Life has become richer by the love that has been lost.

因为失去的爱情   223.
生命变得更丰盈

My friend, your great heart shone with the sunrise
of the East like the snowy summit of a lonely hill
in the dawn.

224.　　朋友

你伟大的心在朝阳中闪烁

仿佛晨曦中积雪的孤峰之巅

The fountain of death makes the still water of life
play.

死亡之泉让生命的止水不止   225.

Those who have everything but thee, my God, laugh at
those who have nothing but thyself.

226.　　神
　　　　那些除了你什么都有的人
　　　　嘲笑那些除了你什么都没有的人

The movement of life has its rest in its own music.

生命的运动在它自己的音乐里安歇   227.

228.　　踢

只能扬尘

不能收获

Kicks only raise dust and not crops from the earth.

我们的名字

夜晚的波光

消逝没有签字

Our names are the light that glows on the sea
waves at night and then dies without leaving its
signature.

230.   让那些盯着玫瑰花的人啊

        多看着玫瑰的刺吧

Let him only see the thorns who has eyes to see the
rose.

用金子装饰飞鸟的翅膀

飞鸟再也不能翱翔

Set the bird's wings with gold and it will never
again soar in the sky.

232.　　　我们当地的莲花

　　　　　以另外一个叫法

　　　　　在异域的水塘

　　　　　一样甜美地开放

The same lotus of our clime blooms here in the alien
water with the same sweetness, under another name.

由心而观
距离越来越远

233.

In heart's perspective the distance looms large.

234.　　月亮清晖漫天
　　　　暗点全部遮掩

The moon has her light all over the sky, her dark
spots to herself.

别说，"又早晨了"   235.
别用一个早已用过的名字
见每个早晨如同初相见
如见一个还没有名字的孩子

Do not say,"It is morning," and dismiss it with a
name of yesterday. See it for the first time as a
new-born child that has no name.

236.   烟对天吹牛逼

          灰对地吹牛逼

          它们是火的兄弟

Smoke boasts to the sky, and Ashes to the earth,
that they are brothers to the fire.

雨滴对茉莉耳语

"永远放我在心底"

茉莉叹了口气

落进泥里

The raindrop whispered to the jasmine,

"Keep me in your heart for ever."

The jasmine sighed, "Alas,"

and dropped to the ground.

238.   胆怯的念头啊
        别怕
        我是一个诗人

Timid thoughts, do not be afraid of me.
I am a poet.

我心念幽暗的静寂中　　239.
似乎充满了蟋蟀的叫声
声音的幽暗的微明

The dim silence of my mind seems filled with
crickets' chirp——the grey twilight of sound.

240.　　　火箭

　　　你向星星挑战

　　　你摔回了地面

Rockets, your insult to the stars follows yourself
back to the earth.

在您的引领下
我穿越白昼中纷繁的俗务
止于我夜幕中的孤独

我等着夜晚的静寂
告诉我这孤独的意义

Thou hast led me through my crowded travels of the
day to my evening's loneliness.
I wait for its meaning through the stillness of the
night.

242.　　　度过一生如同越过汪洋
　　　　　我们碰巧在一条船上

　　　　　死时我们行到海岸
　　　　　然后去各自的下一站

This life is the crossing of a sea, where we meet in
the same narrow ship.
In death we reach the shore and go to our different
worlds.

真理的河 243.

在它谬误的河渠中流过

The stream of truth flows through its channels of
mistakes.

244.   今天我的心止不住思念
          时间之海的一小时甜甜

My heart is homesick to-day for the one sweet hour
across the sea of time.

鸟儿的歌唱

大地对晨曦的回响

The bird-song is the echo of the morning light back
from the earth.

246.   "你骄傲到不愿意亲我？"

晨曦问毛茛

"Are you too proud to kiss me?" the morning light
asks the buttercup.

"太阳啊，我如何歌唱如何崇拜你啊？"小花问

"用你纯洁的静默就够了。"太阳答

"How may I sing to thee and worship, O Sun?"

asked the little flower.

"By the simple silence of thy purity,"

answered the sun.

Man is worse than an animal when he is an animal.

248.　　　人变成禽兽时

　　　　禽兽不如

Dark clouds become heaven's flowers when kissed by
light.

黑云被光吻了   249.
变成天堂之花

Let not the sword-blade mock its handle for being
blunt.

250.   剑锋还是不要嘲笑剑柄的厚钝

The night's silence, like a deep lamp, is burning
with the light of its milky way.

夜晚的静默如同一盏深灯　　251.
亮着银河的星光

Around the sunny island of Life swells day and night
death's limitless song of the sea.

252.　　　阳光灿烂的生命之岛

无尽的死亡之歌日夜环绕

Is not this mountain like a flower, with its petals
of hills, drinking the sunlight?

难道山不像花朵吗   253.
山峰如花瓣
日光浇灌

The real with its meaning read wrong and emphasis
misplaced is the unreal.

254.   "真实"

            意思被误读，轻重被错置

            "不真实"

Find your beauty,
my heart, from the world's movement,
like the boat that has the grace of the wind and the
water.

我的心啊

在世界的运动中找到你的美吧

仿佛船在风和水中的优雅

256.　　眼睛不以视力为傲
　　　　而以眼镜为傲

The eyes are not proud of their sight but of their
eyeglasses.

我生活在我窄小的世界

生怕它变得更小一点点

让我升到你的世界

让我有自由欢快地失去一切

I live in this little world of mine and am afraid to
make it the least less. Lift me into thy world and
let me have the freedom gladly to lose my all.

The false can never grow into truth by growing in
power.

258.   谬误的力量再增长

        也长不成真理

My heart, with its lapping waves of song, longs to
caress this green world of the sunny day.

我的心

随着它浪涌的乐音

渴望抚摸这阳光之下的绿色天地

259.

Wayside grass, love the star, then your dreams will
come out in flowers.

260.   路边的草
       爱上星星吧
       花就梦一样地开了

Let your music, like a sword,
pierce the noise of the market to its heart.

让你的音乐如同利剑   261.

刺穿尘世的喧嚣

直捅心间

The trembling leaves of this tree touch my heart
like the fingers of an infant child.

262.   颤抖的树叶触摸我的心房
        如同一个婴儿的指掌

The sadness of my soul is her bride's veil.

It waits to be lifted in the night.

我消魂的黯然是新娘的面纱

等夜晚到来之后再摘下

263.

（在英文原版中，这首诗与第98首相同，这个译本依照原样收录）

The little flower lies in the dust.
It sought the path of the butterfly.

264.　　　小花坠于尘土
　　　　　追随蝴蝶的脚步

I am in the world of the roads.
The night comes. Open thy gate, thou world of the home.

我在到处是路的世上

夜晚降临

请打开你的门吧

我要回家

266.   我唱完你白天的歌曲

夜晚让我擎着你的灯

走过风雨凄迷的道路

I have sung the songs of thy day.

In the evening let me carry thy lamp through the
stormy path.

我没要你走进我的房间   267.
我的情人，请进入我无尽的孤单

I do not ask thee into the house.
Come into my infinite loneliness, my Lover.

268.　　　死亡是生命的一部分

　　　　　就像出生也是

　　　　　抬脚是走路

　　　　　放下也是

Death belongs to life as birth does.
The walk is in the raising of the foot as in the
laying of it down.

在花朵和阳光里   269.

我已掌握了你耳语的简单含义

请再教我你在痛苦和死亡中的语义

I have learnt the simple meaning of thy whispers in

flowers and sunshine——teach me to know thy words in

pain and death.

270.　　　清晨亲吻她的时候已经太迟

　　　　　昨夜的花颤栗

　　　　　叹气

　　　　　零落土里

The night's flower was late when the morning kissed
her, she shivered and sighed and dropped to the
ground.

透过万物的悲伤
我听见永恒之母的哼唱

Through the sadness of all things I hear the
crooning of the Eternal Mother.

272.　　　大地

作为一个生人
我上了你的岸
作为一个客人
我住了你的房
作为一个朋友
我离开你的门

I came to your shore as a stranger, I lived in your house as a guest, I leave your door as a friend, my earth.

我走了   273.

让我的念想伴你

仿佛落日的余光

在星光静寂的边缘上

Let my thoughts come to you, when I am gone, like

the afterglow of sunset at the margin of starry

silence.

Light in my heart the evening star of rest and then
let the night whisper to me of love.

274.　　在我心里点燃静息的星光
　　　　然后让夜晚和我轻声说爱

I am a child in the dark.

I stretch my hands through the coverlet of night for

thee, Mother.

黑暗中

我就是个儿童

手伸出夜色的被子找

妈妈

The day of work is done. Hide my face in your arms, Mother.

Let me dream.

276.　　白天的活儿干完啦
　　　　我的脸藏进你的臂弯
　　　　妈妈
　　　　让我做梦吧

The lamp of meeting burns long; it goes out in a
moment at the parting.

相见时候   277.

灯一直亮着

一分开就灭了

One word keep for me in thy silence, O World, when I
am dead,"I have loved."

278.　世界啊

我死之后

在你的静默中帮我记住一句话

"我爱过"

We live in this world when we love it.

当我们爱这个世界的时候   279.
我们才活在这个世界上

Let the dead have the immortality of fame, but the
living the immortality of love.

280.　　　让逝者有不朽的名声
　　　　　让生者有不朽的爱情

I have seen thee as the half-awakened child sees his
mother in the dusk of the dawn and then smiles and
sleeps again.

我见过你   281.
仿佛半醒的婴孩
晨曦中看见妈妈
微笑了
又睡了

I shall die again and again to know that life is
inexhaustible.

282.　　　　我将死了又死

　　　　才知道生命不可穷尽

While I was passing with the crowd in the road I saw thy smile from the balcony and I sang and forgot all noise.

我在拥挤的人群穿行   283.

瞥见阳台上你的笑容

我开始歌唱

忘了人来人往

Love is life in its fulness like the cup with its
wine.

284.　　　　爱就是生命的丰满
　　　　　如同酒杯斟满

They light their own lamps and sing their own words
in their temples.
But the birds sing thy name in thine own morning
light,—for thy name is joy.

他们点自己的灯

285.

在自己的庙宇里唱自己的经

飞鸟唱你的名字

在你的晨光里

你的名字就是欢喜

286.
　　领我来到你沉默的中心
　　用歌曲填满我的心

Lead me in the centre of thy silence to fill my heart
with songs.

让他们住在喧嚣的烟花世界中吧

他们自己选了

神啊

我的心渴望你的星辰

287.

Let them live who choose in their own hissing world
of fireworks.
My heart longs for thy stars, my God.

288.　　　爱的痛苦像未知的海

　　　　　　纠缠着我的生活

　　　　　　爱的欢乐像自由的鸟

　　　　　　飞舞在一树树的花开

Love's pain sang round my life like the unplumbed
sea, and love's joy sang like birds in its flowering
groves.

你如果想 289.

就把灯熄了吧

我将理解你的黑暗

我将爱上它

Put out the lamp when thou wishest.

I shall know thy darkness and shall love it.

290.　　白日将尽

我在你面前站立

你将看到我的伤疤

你将了解我的伤以及我疗伤的方法

When I stand before thee at the day's end thou shalt
see my scars and know that I had my wounds and also
my healing.

会有一天

我将在其他世界的日出之时歌唱你

"我在地球的光中见过你

在人类的爱中见过你"

Some day I shall sing to thee in the sunrise of some

other world," I have seen thee before in the light

of the earth, in the love of man."

292.　　　几天前的云飘到我现在的生命里

不再是为了下雨

不再是为了引风

只是为给我落日的天空添彩

Clouds come floating into my life from other days
no longer to shed rain or usher storm but to give
colour to my sunset sky.

真理引发了反对的风暴 293.

种子被风暴吹到天涯海角

Truth raises against itself the storm that scatters
its seeds broadcast.

294.   昨晚的风暴给今早戴上了和平的金冠

The storm of the last night has crowned this morning
with golden peace.

真相似乎有了最后的阐述 295.

这最后的阐述又触发了新的阐述

Truth seems to come with its final word; and the final
word gives birth to its next.

296.　　**实过其名的人**
　　　　有福分

Blessed is he whose fame does not outshine his
truth.

当我忘记我名字的时候

你的名字如蜜糖充盈我的心

如同朝阳消融了雾气

Sweetness of thy name fills my heart when I forget
mine——like thy morning sun when the mist is melted.

298.　　　静寂的夜晚有母亲的美好
　　　　　喧闹的白天有孩子的美好

The silent night has the beauty of the mother and
the clamorous day of the child.

人微笑时

世界爱他

人狂笑时

世界怕他

The world loved man when he smiled. The world became
afraid of him when he laughed.

300.　　　神等着人用智慧

　　　重回童年

God waits for man to regain his childhood in wisdom.

让我感知这个世界

当作你的爱的具象

然后我的爱就能帮忙

Let me feel this world as thy love taking form, then
my love will help it.

302.　你的阳光笑进我心的冬日

让它从不怀疑总会有春花

Thy sunshine smiles upon the winter days of my
heart, never doubting of its spring flowers.

神在爱恋中
亲吻"有限"
人在爱恋中
痴吻"无穷"

God kisses the finite in his love and man the
infinite.

304.　　多年来你穿行荒原

　　　　到达圆满的一瞬间

Thou crossest desert lands of barren years to reach
the moment of fulfilment.

神的无言 305.

让人的思想熟成语言

God's silence ripens man's thoughts into speech.

306.　　　永远在路上的行者

　　　　　你会发现你的脚印都进了我的歌

Thou wilt find, Eternal Traveller, marks of thy
footsteps across my songs.

父亲

您的荣光展现于您的子孙

我不会让您蒙羞

Let me not shame thee, Father, who displayest thy
glory in thy children.

308.　今天很不爽

　　　　愁云压着天光

　　　　仿佛被抽的孩子

　　　　脸蛋儿带着泪光

　　　　风声带着哭腔

　　　　仿佛悲惨世界的哭腔

　　　　但是我知道

　　　　我在去见我朋友的路上

Cheerless is the day, the light under frowning
clouds is like a punished child with traces of
tears on its pale cheeks, and the cry of the wind
is like the cry of a wounded world. But I know I am
travelling to meet my Friend.

今晚

棕榈树叶乱响

海上掀起巨浪

满月如全世界的心悸

从哪个未知天空

你默默地带来了

爱的

痛的

秘密

To-night there is a stir among the palm leaves, a
swell in the sea, Full Moon, like the heart throb of
the world. From what unknown sky hast thou carried
in thy silence the aching secret of love?

310.　　我梦见一颗星

　　　　一个光的岛屿

　　　　我该出生的地点

　　　　在它应接不暇的无尽闲散

　　　　我一生要做的功课渐渐丰满

　　　　仿佛秋日阳光下的稻田

I dream of a star, an island of light, where I shall
be born and in the depth of its quickening leisure
my life will ripen its works like the rice-field in
the autumn sun.

雨中尘土的香　　　　　　　　311.

嘹亮的颂扬

无声的渺小

无尽的聚响

The smell of the wet earth in the rain rises like a
great chant of praise from the voiceless multitude
of the insignificant.

312.　　　爱会消逝

　　　一个我们不愿认作真相的事实

That love can ever lose is a fact that we cannot
accept as truth.

某一天我们会懂得   313.

灵魂所得

死不可夺

因为灵魂和所得已经合成了一个

We shall know some day that death can never rob us

of that which our soul has gained, for her gains are

one with herself.

314.　　　神
　　　　来到我的黄昏
　　　　提篮里鲜嫩着我旧日的花魂

God comes to me in the dusk of my evening with the
flowers from my past kept fresh in his basket.

主啊

当我命中的琴弦都调好

随便一拨

都是爱的曲调

When all the strings of my life will be tuned, my
Master, then at every touch of thine will come out
the music of love.

316.　　　主啊

　　　让我本色地生活

　　　于是死亡也真实了

Let me live truly, my Lord, so that death to me
become true.

人类的历史在耐心期冀　　　　317.
那些被侮辱的人的胜利

Man's history is waiting in patience for the triumph
of the insulted man.

318.　　　此刻我感到

　　　你注视着我的心

　　　仿佛晨光下的静寂

　　　注视着收割之后孤零零的土地

I feel thy gaze upon my heart this moment like the
sunny silence of the morning upon the lonely field
whose harvest is over.

我渴望

喧嚣嘶叫的海里

歌声的岛屿

I long for the Island of Songs across this heaving

Sea of Shouts.

320.　　　夕阳的音乐声中夜色开始弥漫

　　　　　弥漫于庄严的颂歌

　　　　　向不可言说的黑暗

The prelude of the night is commenced in the music
of the sunset, in its solemn hymn to the ineffable
dark.

我曾登上山顶

名声之巅的荒芜不让我得安宁

导师，领我，在天光消失之前

去宁静的山谷

生活的收获圆熟成金色的智珠

I have scaled the peak and found no shelter in
fame's bleak and barren height. Lead me, my Guide,
before the light fades, into the valley of quiet
where life's harvest mellows into golden wisdom.

322.　黄昏的暗淡中
　　　事物变得迷离
　　　塔失去塔基
　　　树尖如墨迹

　　　我等待明天来临
　　　看到光明里你的城市

Things look phantastic in this dimness of the dusk—
the spires whose bases are lost in the dark and tree
tops like blots of ink. I shall wait for the morning
and wake up to see thy city in the light.

我曾受罪

我曾绝望

我曾了解死亡

我欢喜

我在这个伟大的世界上

I have suffered and despaired and known death and I
am glad that I am in this great world.

324.　　　我生命中有些地方

　　　　　寂寥

　　　　　荒凉

　　　　　在这些空旷

　　　　　我的忙碌日子吸收空气和光

There are tracts in my life that are bare and
silent. They are the open spaces where my busy days
had their light and air.

放了我吧   325.

我没实现的昨天

从背后纠缠

让死都变得困难

Release me from my unfulfilled past clinging to me
from behind making death difficult.

326.　　　这是我最后的交代
　　　　　我坚信你的爱

Let this be my last word, that I trust in thy love.

翻译泰戈尔《飞鸟集》的二十七个刹那

1 /

中国传统培养文人的指导思想是：培养出的文人应该是严格意义上的通才，可以从事各种职业，地方官吏、盐铁专卖、纪检监察，甚至包括制造武器、修筑大坝等等理工科技术要求很高的职业。

对于偏文科的职业，培养出的文人运用常识、逻辑、对于人性的洞察，上手几个月可以粗通，干了两三年可以小成，磨砺七八年成为干将。对于理工科技术要求很高的职业，作为通才的文人通过选、用、育、留专业技术人员也可以完成。

通才的培养看上去虚，但也有相当的讲究，常用的纬度可以归纳为管事、管人、管自己。管事和管人不容易，涉及常识、逻辑，把事儿想明白、说清楚，让一个团队听话、出活儿，都是需要修炼的地方，以德服人或者以缺德服人都不容易，所以《红楼梦》里强调"世事洞明皆学问，人情练达即文章"。管自己更难，如何发挥自己的潜能、驾驭自己的欲望、管理自己的情绪等等，是需要几十万字解释的东西，所以"修身齐家治国平天下"中第一位、第一步是修自己的身，对自己狠。

有意思的是，MBA 的教育原则和麦肯锡的培养原则也是：经理人应该是严格意义上的通才，管理本身是种通用于诸多行业的手艺。

古今中外，小二十年学习、实践下来，"为师、为相、为将"，我似乎也成了个放到哪里都能撅着屁股干的通才。

但是，有两个职业，我坚定地认为，我干不了。不是不会干，是太难，干着太痛苦。

一个干不了的职业是律师。在几个场合中深度接触律师后，我才发现，律师能罗列出那么多小概率事件，在这些小概率事件中，人性能呈现出那么丰富的阴暗。硬着头皮做十年律师之后，我再闭门写小说，估计小说里面的无尽黑暗会淹没曾经是柔软的无尽光明；我再出门干俗务，估计管理风格中的以德服人都换成了以缺德服人。

另一个干不了的职业是翻译。语言是人类发明的最具欺骗性的工具，文化是某个人类种群最大的信息聚合，翻译是用最具欺骗性的工具在两个信息之海中间架一座准确、通畅、景色优美的桥。

翻译做多了，我担心我出现精神症状。

2 /

一直负责出版我简体中文书的小孙忽然问我：冯唐老师，您想不想翻译泰戈尔的《飞鸟集》？给您最高标准的翻译费，每个字很多钱。

我想都没想就答应了。

后来，一边翻译，一边想到了一些原因。

比如，小孙勤学上进、靠谱缜密，不会害我。

比如，我刚辞了工作，下一个工作要明年初才开始，正好可以做些稍
稍从容的事情。过去十五年，每次都是一年捞到几天，这几天就是拼
命写小说。

比如，认真的写作者和职业运动员也有相似之处，也需要严格的常
规训练。一本本写小说，就像运动员的"以练代训"，不是说不可以，
而是加上常规训练就更好。对于写作者，我能想象的最好的常规训练
莫过于用现代汉语翻译经典古代汉语、用现代汉语翻译经典西方文
章，用更少的字数，不失原文的意境和汁液。

比如，泰戈尔得过诺贝尔奖，我想知道，一百年前，政治味道不浓的
时候，给东方的诺贝尔奖是什么味道。

比如，流行译本的作者郑振铎是民国摇曳的人物之一，少年时代我仔细
读过《西谛书话》，我想就着他的翻译走到民国，掂掂那时的月色风声。
我坚信民国时代的中文还在转型期，我现在有能力把中文用得更好。

比如，我是中文超简诗派创始人，诗歌长度通常比唐诗七律、七绝、
五律、五绝还短。据说《飞鸟集》也是浓缩得不能再浓缩的诗集，我
想仔细见识一下。

比如，小孙说，最高的翻译费，每个字很多钱。从少年时代起，我就幻想着能靠码字过上自由自在的生活，不知道过了这么多年，幻想是不是还是幻想。

3 /

幻想还是幻想，幻想很快落空了。《飞鸟集》字数出奇地少，如果我在一万个汉字之内翻译不完，是我的耻辱，我对不起汉语，请借我一把割腕或者剖腹用的蒙古刀。

但是既然答应翻译了，就尊重契约精神，翻译下去。

4 /

小孙给我寄来了泰戈尔的原本。小孙讲究，说：这样，冯译《飞鸟集》在版权页上就可以清晰标注：译自 Forgotten Books 出版社 2012 年重印本。

5 /

我在加州湾区纳帕附近租了个民房——一个纯美国老太太很早之前买的。那时候，附近的海军基地还没废弃，修船厂船来船往，很热闹。如今冷清了，废弃基地的一部分活化成了滨海公园，可以跑步，可以听海，可以体会空寂，间或有警告牌，说：不能再往前了，可能有没清干净的炸弹。

房子不大，院子很大。房子里很多东西，粗分两类，比美国老太太还老的东西和没美国老太太老但是她舍不得丢掉的东西。院子里很多香草、薄荷、薰衣草、鼠尾草、百里香、迷迭香，还有不少果树，柠檬、橘子、无花果，还有片小菜地，西红柿、茄子、不知名的瓜，还有完全不修整的芭蕉、完全自由的紫色牵牛花、完全想来就来想走就走的野猫，五组椅子——一天中随着太阳和风的变化，人可以变化自己屁股的位置。

我找了半天形容词来总结这个院子，没得逞。偶尔听到一个意大利人的用词，"有组织的杂乱"，贴切。

贴地面运动的是蚂蚁。人坐着的时候，沿着人的鞋子和裤子爬进人的身体。意识不到的时候，无所谓；感到了，一个冷颤，尽管不知道冷颤个什么。

齐身体高低运动的是苍蝇、蜜蜂、松鼠和小鸟。他们围着植物的花和果实忙碌，不知道它们何时生、何时死，估计它们自己也不知道，也不想知道。太阳出来了，还能忙碌，就是赚了。

高过头顶运动的是风。不知道它从何处来，不知道它去向何处，不知道它现在要干吗。但是，风拨动树叶，不同角度、力度、持续时间，发出细碎的声音，从不重复，我听一两个小时也不会烦。风敲响挂在屋檐下的风铃，昼夜不停，睡前是它，睡醒是它，梦里是它，真好听，日本京都精于禅宗音乐的和尚也敲不出。

高过房顶的是云。它想变成啥样子就变成啥样子，我去冰箱里又开了一瓶不同牌子的当地啤酒，再回到院子，它又变了一个姿势给我看。

果树长满了果实，没人摘，蚁过、猫过、风过、云过，熟透的果实脱落，砸在地上，皮球一样，人头一样，所有躲不开的事情一样。

6 /

刚开始翻译就出现问题。

郑振铎旧译总体偏平实，但是集子题目反而翻得飘。《Stray Birds》翻译为《飞鸟集》，从英文字面和里面多数诗歌的指向，翻译成《迷鸟集》或者《失鸟集》似乎更好。

想了想，还是决定保留《飞鸟集》这个名字。几个原因：《飞鸟集》已经被中文读者所熟知；"迷鸟"或者"失鸟"不是已知汉语词汇，"飞鸟"是；我喜欢的诗人李白写过一句我喜欢的诗，"众鸟高飞尽，孤云独去闲"。

据说，鸟从来不迷路，鸟善于利用太阳、星辰、地球磁场等等现成的伟大事物随时帮助自己确定方向。

人才常常迷路。

7 /

郑振铎的序言里说，泰戈尔最初的著作都是用孟加拉文写的，比之后的英文翻译更加美丽。

我没问到，泰戈尔的孟加拉文诗歌是否押韵。但是泰戈尔的英文翻译是不押韵的，郑振铎的汉语翻译是不押韵的，无论英文还是中文都更像剥到骨髓的散文。

我固执地认为，诗应该押韵。诗不押韵，就像姑娘没头发一样别扭。不押韵的一流诗歌即使勉强算作诗，也不如押韵的二流诗歌。我决定，我的译本尽全力押韵。

翻译过程中发现，这个决定耗掉了我大量精力，翻译中一半的时间是在寻找最佳的押韵。

在寻找韵脚的过程中，我越来越坚信，押韵是诗人最厉害的武器。

有了押韵，诗人就可以征服世界去了。

"天子呼来不上船，笑称臣是酒中仙。"

8 /

翻译第一首的时候，就遇到一个困难的权衡。

英文原文是：

Stray birds of summer come to my window to sing and fly away.

And yellow leaves of autumn, which have no songs, flutter and fall
there with a sigh.

一种翻译风格可以更贴近中国古体诗，可以更整洁：

夏日飞鸟
我窗鸣叫
敛歌而消

秋天黄叶
无翼无啸
坠地而憔

另一种翻译风格可以更贴近现代诗，可以更缭绕：

夏日的飞鸟来到我窗前
歌
笑
翩跹
消失在我眼前

秋天的黄叶一直在窗前
无歌
无笑
无翩跹
坠落在我眼前

斟酌再三，选择了后一种作为翻译《飞鸟集》的整体风格。最主要的
原因是，现在是现代了。

9 /

翻译完五十首之后，我开始怀疑我是不是适合翻译《飞鸟集》。我的
风格是行神如空、行气如虹，"罗襦宝带为君解，燕歌赵舞为君开"。
相比之下，《飞鸟集》似乎太软了，泰戈尔似乎太软了，似乎由徐志
摩、谢冰心、戴望舒、张恨水、汪国真、董桥等"碧桃满树，风日水
滨"的前辈们来翻译更合适。

再翻译一百首之后，我觉得我错了，我还是适合翻译《飞鸟集》的。

第一，小溪和瀑布是不一样的，池塘和大海是不一样的。有些作者表
面看着温软，实际上也是温软。有些作者表面看着温软，但是内心强
大、金刚智慧，太极拳也能一招制敌。泰戈尔是后者。

比如，《飞鸟集》第七十一首：

> 砍树的铁斧向树要木头把儿
> 树给了它

第二，每个人，包括我，都有柔软的部分。我也喜欢早上下一阵小雨，
也喜欢小男孩、小女孩紧紧拽着我的手去看他们想让我看的东西。

翻译的一瞬间，我也回想起了二十多年前，我和我初恋，在一个屋子

里抱在一起，从早到晚，三十多天，尽管我们都学过了《生理卫生》，仍然一直穿着衣服，一直什么也没做。

如果不是翻译《飞鸟集》，我都忘了，我曾经那么纯洁。

10 /

出书的时候，我会和出版商建议，哪怕诗再短，也要一首占一页，多余的空间就空在那里，仿佛山水画中的留白。

读最好的短诗，需要留白，需要停顿，需要长长叹一口气，然后再接着读下一首，仿佛亲最好的嘴唇，需要闭眼，需要停顿，需要长长叹一口气，然后再说："我还要再见你，再见的时候，我还要这样闭上眼睛。"

11 /

和其他类型的创造一样，码字也要在"有我"和"无我"之间寻求平衡。写作应该更偏"无我"一些，最好的写作是老天抓着作者的手码字，作者只是某种媒介而已。翻译应该更"有我"一些，否则，一边是一个悠久文化中的写作大师，另一边是另一个悠久文化的众多经典，没些浑不吝的"有我"劲儿，怎么逢山开道、遇水搭桥？

具体到翻译诗，就需要更加"有我"，力图还魂。在翻译《飞鸟集》的过程中，我没百分之百尊重原文，但是我觉得我有自由平衡信、达、雅。人生事贵快意，何况译诗？

翻译的"有我"之境，不只是译者的遣词、造句、布局、押韵，更是译者的见识、敏感、光明、黑暗。

《飞鸟集》第十二首，粗看英文原文和中文译文都不抓人：

"沧海，你用的是哪种语言？"
"永不止息的探问。"
"苍天，你用的是哪种语言？"
"永不止息的沉默。"

翻译的刹那，我想起我和我初恋之间很多很平淡无奇的对话。

分手之后很多年，偶尔联系，我总是忍不住问："为什么我们不能在一起？没任何世俗暗示，只是问问。"我初恋总是不答，怎么问，也还是不答。有一阵，我初恋见我之前，都要提醒我："能不能不要问问题了？"我忍住不问了，又过了一阵，就没联系了。

翻译的刹那，我想起我一直没得到回答的问题，我似乎懂了，再也不想问了。

在笔记本上抄了一遍《飞鸟集》第四十二首：

你对我微笑不语
为这句我等了几个世纪

13 /

好的短诗不是对于生活的过度归纳，而是山里的玉石、海里的珍珠。

友人知道我在翻译诗歌，发过来一个截屏：

在这个忧伤而明媚的三月
我从我单薄的青春里打马而过
穿过紫堇
穿过木棉
穿过时隐时现的悲喜和无常

翻译：It's March, I'm a bitch.

这不是好诗，不是好翻译，而是段子手对于生活过度的归纳。

同样字数少，"陌上花开，可缓缓归"是好的短诗。

14 /

更多"神译"在我翻译《飞鸟集》的过程中被转来。

We Are the Champions，我们都是昌平人；We Found Love，潍坊的爱；Young Girls，秧歌；Open Heart，开心；Because You Love Me，因为你是我的优乐美；We Need Medicine，我们不能放弃治疗；Wake Me Up When September Ends，一觉睡到国庆节；The Best of the Yardbirds，绝

味鸭脖；Follow Your Heart，怂；等等。

这些和好翻译没有关系，就像小聪明和大智慧没有关系。

《飞鸟集》第九十六首是这样说的：

> 此时的噪音
> 嘲笑永恒的乐音

15 /

有些诗的好处在于拿捏准确。

比如《飞鸟集》第十九首：

> 神啊
> 我的欲念如此纷纷扰扰呆痴憨傻
> 好吧
> 我只是听听吧

我对妄念的定义是：如果你有一个期望，这个期望长期挥之不去，而且需要别人来满足，这个期望就是妄念。

有些时候，一些妄念莫名其妙地升起。你知道是妄念，但是你不知道这些妄念为什么升起，也不知道这些妄念会到哪里去。多数时候，你无法阻止妄念升起，就像你无法阻止你的屎意和尿意。多数时候，你也不应该被这些妄念挟持，做出无数后悔的事儿。

合适的态度就像这首诗里的态度，既然被神这么设计我们了，既然这种设计会让我们有妄念产生，那就找个安静的地方，听听妄念如何唠叨，看看妄念如何雾散云消。

16 /

有些诗的好处在于三观贴心。

比如《飞鸟集》第二十首：

> 我做不到选择最好的
> 是最好的选择了我

这种态度里面满满的是自信、乐观、顺应、坦然。既然生为一朵花，那就别总想着最好是生为一朵花、一棵草，还是一棵树，对你而言，成为一朵花就是最好的。

17 /

有些诗的好处在于解决现实问题。

我进入大学之后，一路追求"第一、唯一、最"，一味迷信只问耕耘、不问收获，生活简单、思想复杂，行万里路、读万卷书，一周工作八十小时以上，一年飞十万公里以上，在吃苦的过程中获得一种苦行的快感。看着这个"我"越来越锋利，常常内心肿胀地背诵那首古诗："十年磨一剑，霜刃未曾试。今日把示君，谁有不平事？"

后来经历的事儿多了些，隐约觉得这种执着中有非常不对的东西，锋利不该是全部，一个人能左右的东西其实也不多。

翻译《飞鸟集》第四十五首，心里释然了很多：

> 他尊他的剑为神
> 剑胜了
> 他输了

18 /

湾区的夏天很冷，最热的天儿，下水游泳也冻得慌，马克·吐温甚至说过"我所经历过最冷的冬天就是旧金山的夏天"。

但是靠近中午的时候，大太阳出来，天可以变得挺热，我就把电脑和书搬出来，坐在院子阴凉的地方，吹风、看云、听树、译诗。

在户外译诗的好处是，诗变成一种很自然的东西，仿佛风动、云卷、树摇、猫走、雨来，人硬造的棱角减少，塑料花慢慢有了些真花的风致。

太阳快熄灭的时候，晚霞满天，不似人间。用院子里杂木的枯枝和网购包装纸箱点起一盆篝火，院子里又能多坐一会儿了。掐一把鼠尾草和薰衣草放在火盆罩上，开一瓶红酒放在手边，又能多翻译好几首诗了。

月有阴晴圆缺，小说有起承转合，一本诗集也有高峰和低谷，《飞鸟集》似乎也不例外，翻译到中间，不少诗平平。

烤鸭不都是皮，大师也是人，泰戈尔也不是神。

20 /

诗常常因为用词单一和意境单调受人攻击。

网上流传，唐诗基本总结为：田园有宅男，边塞多愤青。咏古伤不起，送别满基情。人妻空房守，浪子卧青楼。去国伤不起，满怀平戎忧。宋词基本总结为：小资喝花酒，老兵坐床头，知青咏古自助游。皇上宫中愁，剩女宅家里，萝莉嫁王侯，名媛丈夫死得早，妹妹在青楼。

《飞鸟集》里频繁出现的是：花、草、树、天、地、海、人、神、夜、晨、星、月、日、风、雨、泪、笑、歌、心、诗、灯、窗。

但是，转一个角度，从更正面的角度想这种单一和单调，一生不长，重要的事儿也没那么多，《飞鸟集》中涉及的这些不多的简单的东西，恰恰构成生命中最重要的部分。

我一直生活、工作在大城市，最常做的运动是：开会、思考、看书、喝茶、饮酒，从来不认为自己可以长时间待在非大城市的地方。在纳帕乡间翻译《飞鸟集》，让我第一次意识到，大城市也不是必需，有

了花、草、树、天、地、海、人、神、夜、晨、星、月、日、风、
雨、泪、笑、歌、心、诗、灯、窗，就很好了。

21 /

《飞鸟集》三百二十五首短诗，完全没顺序，和《论语》一样。

细想，生命不是也一样？

22 /

郑振铎，一八九八年十二月十九日生，二十几岁翻译《飞鸟集》，不
求押韵，但是基本没有翻译错误，平顺中正。

我们这一辈、我们上一辈、我们下一辈，二十几岁的时候，都干什么
去了？

23 /

在翻译《飞鸟集》第二百一十九首的时候，我第一次也是唯一一次觉
得郑振铎的翻译出现了明显问题。

原文：Men are cruel, but Man is kind.
郑译：独夫们是凶暴的，但人民是善良的。

感到两个问题。第一是，Men 为什么译为"独夫们"（又，既然是独

夫，何来"们"）？ Man 为什么译为"人民"？第二是，即使词没译错，总体意思出现了常识问题。独夫的确残暴，但是独夫统治下的人民从来就不是善良的，如果不是大部分不善良，也一定不是大部分善良。否则，独夫的力量从哪里来？纳粹在欧洲，日本兵在南京，大部分都不是善良的。这些成群结队的"人民"，灭绝人性时，没体现出任何善良，而且在过程中坚信自己是正确的。

我的体会，这首诗揭示的是众人和个体之间的巨大差异。个体的人性中，有善、有恶、有神圣，单一个体容易平衡，很难呈现大恶，即使出现，也会被其他人迅速扑灭，不会造成大害。而聚合成组织，个体的恶有可能被集中放大、被管理者利用，形成大恶。一旦集体意志形成，机器开动，个体无助，或被机器消灭，或成为机器的一部分，去消灭他人。从这个角度观照，Men 指某些人的聚合，指团队、政党、政权等等，Man 指人性，你、我、他、她，每个个体展现的人性。

翻译的时候，我想了很久，简单的译法是：众人是残酷的，人性是善良的。

但是最后译成：庸众是残酷的，每个人是善良的。

只有庸众而不是普通群众才是残酷的，庸众的特征是唯利是从、唯权是从、唯捷径是从、唯成功是从，无论什么样的当权者，只要是当权者说的，都是对的。无论是非曲折，只要有人倒霉，特别是似乎过得比自己好的人倒霉，就会叫好。人性本善，不错，但是这首诗强调的是个体，重点不在善，翻译成每个人更警世。而且，每个人加在一起就是人类，每个人都有的，就是人性。

译完，想起在"二战"的德国、红色高棉的柬埔寨，庸众的所作所为，愣了很久，发了个微博："翻译《飞鸟集》第 219 首：'Men are cruel, but Man is kind.' / '庸众是残酷的，每个人是善良的'……简单一句话，想了很久。"

此微博，评论超四百个，转发近一千五百次，阅读一百五十万次。有指点的、有挖苦的、有显摆学问的、有手痒自己重译的，好久没看到众人对一句英文这么认真了，真好。

大学英文系教授朱绩崧（文冤阁大学士）数条微博和微信赐教："拙译：恶者虽众，人性本善。用'众'和'人'分别对应 Men 和 Man。"

"语言的本质是分类系统，不同的语言就是不同的分类系统。跨语种的翻译（interlingual translation）本来就是在不同的分类系统之间做出的近似匹配，严丝密缝的吻合是奇迹，可遇不可求。所以，翻译的常态只能是妥协，绝不是完美。"

我回："感谢指点。翻译原则不一定只有一套，信达雅在具体位置上如何平衡，译者有一定的自主权。人生事贵快意，何况译诗？诗意不只是在翻译中失去的，诗意也可以是在翻译中增加的，仿佛酒倒进杯子。"

24 /

英文原版出现了一个排版错误，第二百六十三首和第九十八首完全重复；郑译本已经纠正了。

25 /

在翻译完成前几天，地震了，震中就在纳帕，六级。我出门去南边，没在。夜里还是被震醒。想起湾区房子都是木头做的，就又倒头睡了。

新闻里说，纳帕已经二十五年没大地震了，很多酒庄的存酒都被毁了，酒桶滚了一地，酒瓶子碎了一地。

26 /

我有个公众微信号：fengtang1971。欢迎词是这样写的：欢迎，欢迎，热烈欢迎。冯唐读诗，冯唐诗、唐诗、诗经、现代诗、外国诗。偶尔发冯唐杂文，更偶尔发冯唐照的照片。诗不当吃喝，但是诗是我们生活的必需。不着急，不害怕，且读诗，且饮酒。"读诗再睡教"。

我自己的诗早就读完了。翻译《飞鸟集》之后，我开始在微信公众号上每天读一首《飞鸟集》中的短诗，先英文原文，再冯唐翻译，偶尔加入我的简短解读。

有人讽刺我英文发音，我觉得还是坚持我的北京腔英文。留下几个吐槽点，听众容易快乐。

有人把微信语音转文字的功能用在我的公众微信上，因为里面有北京腔的中文、英文和偶尔的结巴，翻译出的文字多类似如下：

罗宾德拉纳特·泰戈尔

Rabindranath Tagore

1861–1941

印度诗人、哲学家、教育家、社会活动家

印度近代中短篇小说创始人

1913 年，成为第一位获得诺贝尔文学奖的亚洲人

代表作品

诗集

1910 年《吉檀迦利》

1913 年《新月集》《园丁集》

1916 年《飞鸟集》

1928 年《流萤集》

小说

1894 年《太阳与乌云》

1906 年《沉船》

1910 年《戈拉》

剧作

1911 年《顽固堡垒》

1922 年《摩克多塔拉》

1926 年《人红夹竹桃》

散文

1881 年《死亡的贸易》

1924 年《中国的谈话》

1931 年《俄罗斯书简》

冯 唐

1971 年生于北京，男，诗人、作家、古器物爱好者
《人民文学》杂志 "未来大家" TOP20 之首

1998 年，获中国协和医科大学临床医学博士学位
2000 年，获美国 Emory University 工商管理硕士
2000-2008 年，麦肯锡公司全球董事合伙人
2009-2014 年，某大型医疗集团创始 CEO
如今，自由写作、风险投资

已出版作品

长篇小说《欢喜》
长篇小说《十八岁给我一个姑娘》
长篇小说《万物生长》
长篇小说《北京，北京》
随笔集《活着活着就老了》
诗集《冯唐诗百首》
长篇小说《不二》
随笔集《三十六大》
长篇小说《女神一号》

微博 http://weibo.com/fengtang
微信公共账号 fengtang1971

果麦

飞鸟集

产品经理 | 孙雪净

责任编辑 | 金荣良　装帧设计 | 介太书衣

后期制作 | 顾利军　责任印制 | 蒋建浩　特约印制 | 刘淼

媒介推广 | 金锐　何婷　特约发行 | 王誉　柴贵满

策划人 | 吴畏

官方网站 http://www.guomai.cc
官方微博 http://weibo.com/gmguomai
官方天猫店 http://guomaits.tmall.com

图书在版编目（CIP）数据

飞鸟集 / (印) 泰戈尔著 ; 冯唐译. -- 杭州 : 浙
江文艺出版社, 2015.7
　　ISBN 978-7-5339-4075-1

　　Ⅰ. ①飞… Ⅱ. ①泰… ②冯… Ⅲ. ①诗集 – 印度 –
现代 Ⅳ. ①I351.25

中国版本图书馆CIP数据核字(2014)第280556号

责任编辑　金荣良
装帧设计　介太书衣

飞鸟集
〔印度〕罗宾德拉纳特·泰戈尔　著
冯唐　译

出版　浙江出版联合集团
　　　浙江文艺出版社

地址　杭州市体育场路347号　　邮编　310006
网址　www.zjwycbs.cn
经销　浙江省新华书店集团有限公司
印刷　北京旭丰源印刷技术有限公司
开本　880mm×1230mm　1/32
字数　22千字
印张　11.25
插页　5
版次　2015年7月第1版　2015年7月第1次印刷
书号　ISBN 978-7-5339-4075-1
定价　39.00元